Get Me to School!

Written by Nancy O'Connor

Flying Start
to Literacy®

T0363465

Contents

Introduction

The next time your alarm goes off and you wish it was Saturday because you'd rather not go to school, think of all the children who can't go to school.

You might not know this, but in 2015, it was estimated that more than 61 million primary school-aged children around the world weren't attending school.

Fun fact

To give you an idea of how big a number 61 million is, if all those children held hands and formed a human chain, they would circle the globe one and a half times!

Primary school children, Pakistan. Most girls do not go on to secondary school in Pakistan.

The main reason why children don't go to school is that they don't have schools or they can't afford a teacher. And in some countries, there are wars or **famines**. Some children are forbidden to attend school simply because they are girls.

An education means a better future, and in places around the world where it's hard to get an education, many people are trying to make sure that kids don't miss out!

Chapter 1

No easy way there!

For many children around the world, a long and difficult journey to school and back is common. This might mean setting off at five o'clock in the morning, while it is still dark, and not returning home until seven at night.

For these children, riding in a car or catching a bus is hard to imagine, but what they all have in common is that they *really* want to learn.

Young students in Cuba ride in the back of donkey carts.

These children are crossing a hanging bridge in the Himalayan mountains to get to school.

Zip lines

Can you imagine getting to school by **zip line**? Nine-year-old Daisy Mora must do that every day to reach her school in the jungle. She lives in a remote part of Colombia, a country in South America.

A zip line made of wire cables stretches across a canyon and is the only way the people from her village can connect with the outside world.

This may sound fun and exciting, but the canyon is about 400 metres deep, with a rushing river at the bottom! Daisy sits in a sling that hangs from the cables. Her five-year-old brother, Jamid, is too young to make the ride by himself, so he rides with Daisy in a **jute** sack.

The cable is almost one kilometre long. Passengers travel at 60 kilometres an hour to reach the other side.

Daisy and her brother Jamid travel to school by zip line.

River rafts

In Indonesia, children often use homemade bamboo rafts to cross rivers so they can reach their schools.

Others walk through rice fields. Sometimes, when it's especially muddy, they take off their shoes and hold them high over their heads. When they arrive at school, the students wash their legs and feet, put on their clean shoes and are ready to learn.

Chapter 2

Travelling schools

Would you like to attend school on a boat?
Or go to a donkey library?

In some places, the best way to help children
get an education is to bring the classroom
or the library to them.

These children in Indonesia are using
a traditional boat to get to their school.

Boat schools

The country of Bangladesh in Southeast Asia has a four-month **monsoon season** every year. Heavy rains flood many of the roads, keeping millions of children from getting to school.

But a man named Mohammed Rezwan thought, *Why not have schools travel to them?* Mohammed, who is an architect, decided to build some boat schools.

These boats serve as both school buses and classrooms. They float down the flooded rivers, picking up students along the way. Then each boat school ties up to a dock and the day's lessons begin. Some of the boats house libraries. Others are solar-powered computer labs. There are even boats that are filled with play equipment – a floating playground!

At the end of the day, the boats return students to their homes. Each child leaves with a **solar** lantern to help them to do their schoolwork after dark. Mohammed's idea has been so successful that floating schools are now also found in Cambodia, Vietnam and other flood-prone parts of the world.

Students in Bangladesh

Biblioburro

For over 20 years, a former teacher named Luis Soriano has travelled with his two **burros** to remote villages in Colombia, a country in South America. Packs filled with books of all kinds are strapped to their sides.

Starting out with only 70 precious books, Luis has shared his love of reading with thousands of children. Many of them had never before held a book until Luis and his burros arrived.

Luis with his burros, which are named Alfa and Beto.

Being a travelling librarian is not an easy job. Some villages are many kilometres from Luis's home. He often has to travel through jungles where there are dangerous animals. Sometimes, bandits have made his mission dangerous. Once he was even held **hostage**, but his captors were disappointed to find that the burros' packs held only books. They had hoped for something more valuable, so they quickly released him. Luis, of course, didn't admit how valuable those books were to him and all the village children!

These days, Luis's library contains over 5,000 books, and he has several people who help him. Besides sharing books, Luis has taught many village children how to read and write. He has always had only two rules for those wanting to use the library – to wash their hands before handling a book and never to write on the pages. He is especially proud of Leticia, one of his best students. She grew up to become a primary school librarian.

Chapter 3

Caves and train platforms

If there is no school for children to go to, why not create one where they are? After all, a school isn't just a building; it's a place where there are children and someone to teach them.

Cave school

Imagine going to school in a cave. Children in a small village in the mountains of China did that for many years.

This primary school in China was inside a cave.

The cave school even had a basketball court.

Mid-Cave Primary School opened in 1984 with eight teachers and 186 students. The cave was so huge that people from the village built several wooden classrooms inside it. The classrooms didn't need to have roofs because the cave protected them from the wind and rain. There was even a playground and a basketball court. The stone walls of the cave were cold, but they helped students learn about rocks and fossils. Plenty of bats and lizards made it interesting for them to study biology!

The cave school was successful, but in 2011, the government decided to close it down. It wanted to build something more modern. Unfortunately, the new modern school is a two-hour walk from the village.

These children in India don't have a school to go to every day.

Train platform schools

In India, millions of children live on the streets. Many may be runaways or orphans, but all are extremely poor.

One teacher, Inderjit Khurana, noticed many of these children gathered at railway stations as she travelled by train back and forth to the primary school where she taught. Some of the children shined the shoes of travellers. Others begged for coins from the people passing by. It was clear to her that they weren't attending school.

Inderjit Khurana with some of her students on a train platform school.

Inderjit believed that these children would never be able to escape **poverty** and homelessness without an education. That gave her an idea. She would create a school just for them – right there in the station!

At first, only about 20 children came to her "train platform school". They gathered around Inderjit and sat on the concrete as train travellers bustled past them.

Word of what she was doing spread, and more children came. She taught reading, maths and healthy living, and she made the learning fun. She played games, sang songs and danced with the children.

Soon, the school became so popular that Inderjit had over 100 students. She had to hire teachers to teach in other train stations.

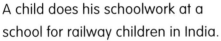

A child does his schoolwork at a
school for railway children in India.

Today, there are more than 70 train platform
schools throughout India. In 2007, Inderjit won
an award in the World's Children's Prize for the
Rights of the Child. She and two of her train
platform students, Bijay and Sanjukta, travelled
all the way to Sweden – halfway around the
world – to receive the award. Imagine how
proud they must have been!

Chapter 4

It's all fun and games!

It doesn't matter where you live, what kind of school you attend or what language you speak, all children enjoy recess. It's a time to have fun with your friends, stretch your legs, improve your sports skills and get physically fit.

What games do you play at recess? Children worldwide play many of the same popular games. They just have different names and different rules for them.

Jump rope

Jump rope and variations of the game are found in many countries.

In the Philippines, however, the game is played with long bamboo sticks. It's called Tinikling, and combines jump rope with dance. Two children sit on the ground and clap the bamboo sticks together in time to a song. Other children jump in between and out of the sticks, almost like double Dutch, which uses two jump ropes.

Tag

Have you ever played tag? It's a popular game in many countries around the world.

In Pakistan, the game of tag is called Oonch Neech. *Oonch* means "up" and *Neech* means "down". If the person who is It calls out *"Oonch"*, no one is safe who is up on the playground equipment, standing on a step or a bench, or clinging to the branch of a tree. If *"Neech"* is called, no one standing on the ground is safe. They must climb up on something before they get tagged. The first child tagged is It for the next round.

These children in England are playing off-the-ground tag.

In Brazil, groups of students play a tag game called Luta de Galo, which means "fight of the roosters". Everyone playing needs a bandana or rag, which they tuck into their belt, pocket or waistband. Pairs compete, trying to steal the bandana of each of their opponents.

But to make the game more difficult, both players must cross their right arm over their chest and lift their left leg. Then they have to hop while trying to grab an opponent's bandana. Players who put down their left foot or uncross their right arm are out of the game.

Conclusion

There are lots of children who are not fortunate enough to receive an education. Even the ones who have to take long and difficult journeys can be considered lucky compared with those who are unable to go to school. There are many who think that this is wrong and that all children should be able to have an education.

Malala Yousafzai is a Pakistani girl who spoke out about her belief that education should be a basic right for all children, even though it was dangerous to do so. When she was just 16, she was awarded a **Nobel Peace Prize** for her efforts – the youngest person to ever receive the prize. She works hard to make sure the message "An education makes a better future" is heard by everyone!

"One child, one teacher, one pen and one book can change the world."

Malala Yousafzai

Glossary

burros the Spanish word for "donkeys"

famines food shortages

hostage a person who has been captured by someone

jute a rough plant fibre

monsoon season a period of heavy rain during summer in southern Asia

Nobel Peace Prize a famous prize that is awarded every year to a person who works for peace in the world

poverty the state of being very poor

solar powered by the sun

zip line a cable a person can ride on to cross between two points

Index